RPMs
A life energized by spinning around Jesus

By Jess G. Strickland

living**hope**

RPMs

Copyright © living**hope** 2011 by Jess G. Strickland

Requests for information should be addressed to:

living**hope** *Aloha, Oregon 97006*

ISBN 978-0-9827364-1-8

Cover photo from Getty Images, by Emma Johnson.

Table of Contents

Acknowledgements

My wife, Brenda, for her constant love, faith, and support. I couldn't do what I do without you.

My children, Jerushah and Jared, for their belief in me, living**hope**, and this project.

My editor Ruth Happ and the entire editing team at living**hope.** Thanks for making me look good.

Amy Wheelon for cover art work, and my son Jared for design concepts. It exceeds my expectations.

Foreword

It has been my privilege to know Pastor Jess Strickland for more than thirty years. He has always been a front runner. RPMs describes the way Jess lives his Christian life. He always stretches forward, in this case, to the Lord.

RPMs challenges everyone to expand their faith by reading the Word of God with a Holy Spirit quickening. The Word then moves beyond just a Bible statement to a living Word that causes your faith to want to walk in truth.

If you want to stay alive and well in this day, you must have a daily intake of God's Word. As food is to the natural body, so the Word is for your spirit. Listen and meditate as God speaks to you through His word. Prayer is the wonderful opportunity we have to commune with our Heavenly Father. Don't ever allow the precious to become common and thereby not read the Word, pray, or meditate on the wonderful works of God.

This book will expand your love for God and His Word.

Pastor Dick Iverson
Former Pastor of Bible Temple
Founder of Ministers Fellowship International

Preface

I love riding bikes. When I first started, I purchased one of those computers that told me how fast I was going and how fast I was spinning my revolutions per minute. My goal was to keep my bike in the gear that would allow me to spin between 100 and 110 rpms. Unless I was going downhill, my rpms were what provided movement for my bike.

I have learned over the years that I need spiritual movement. I have also discovered a style of devotions that allows my heart to spin around the Lord at a rate that provides a lifetime of momentum. Before I say much more, let me make it clear that the "style" of devotions is not what has created the energy. It is within the environment of the style that I have encountered the Lord and have been drawn to follow Him in a strength that is not my own. It is my desire to share that style with you (a style I call the "RPMs") in the hope that it will inspire similar results in you.

We live in a world where people are either stagnant with no movement at all or blistering through life at amazing speeds, not realizing their momentum is a lust-filled freefall from the high cliff of gratification. The most fearful aspect of their freefall is that they have not taken time to see the crash they are about to experience. Because of this, they have a similar malady to the stagnant; both are aimless.

Stagnant people are not passionate enough about where they are going to move at all, whereas the freefallers are indifferent about where they are headed. They foolishly avoid looking and calculating the distance to impact. Thomas and Art Rainer define two elements necessary to get things moving: first, you need to act intentionally, and second, you need to act incrementally. I discovered that when I was seeking to get my rpms consistent as a bike rider, I needed to look at my computer often to see how fast I was spinning. Many times I was surprised at how much I had slowed my spin cycle by simply losing concentration. Furthermore, when I first started riding, 100 to 110 rpms were too much for me. So, I began at 85 rpms for my first few long rides, then increased it over a period of months until the 100 to 110 spin cycle felt comfortable. I no longer use a cadence computer. When I drop under 100 rpms, it doesn't feel right.

You can probably see where I am headed with all this. The "RPMs" style of daily walking with Christ is a way to spend time with the Lord in an intentional (calculated) and incremental (step-by-step) way.

Don't be stagnant. Don't freefall over some lust cliff, but let your whole life be changed. Allow your life to start spinning around Christ as you follow Him with all your heart. This book is designed to get you following Jesus in a way that will place the wisdom of heaven within your heart's reach. This book is designed to increase your spin around the Lord and toward your God-destiny, though not as a result of self-effort, but by the grace of God, as Jesus reveals His Gospel and His will to you daily.

Take off with a new energy. Don't walk when you can run; don't run when you can fly. Let Christ grow your trust, releasing you to spin in His Word and giving you momentum to act in obedience.

But those who wait on the Lord shall renew their strength; they shall mount up with wings like eagles, they shall run and not be weary, they shall walk and not faint. Isaiah 40:31 NKJV

Therefore, if anyone is in Christ, he is a new creation; old things have passed away; behold, all things have become new.
1 Corinthians 5:17 NKJV

Think about it. Clock hands spin, wind mills spin, the turbine in a dam spins, wheels spin on their hubs, planets spin around the sun, and the earth spins on its axis. We could talk about atomic energy and electrical energy, but the point is this: spinning produces energy, and the greatest energy of all is when a follower's life is spinning around Jesus Christ. Join us for a great spin class. It will make you mighty in spirit!

Introduction

At living**hope**, we believe that God is into giving people another chance. His design is not perpetual failure. Rather, it is a kind of faith in Him that leads to action, resulting in a changed and blessed life—freedom from patterns of addiction, sorrow, uncertainty, and aimlessness, and into a blessed life. While we are enthusiastic to announce that God wants to give everyone "another chance," we are also dedicated to helping every person make the most of the chance that God (through Christ) is giving him or her.

This book, titled *RPMs*, is designed to get you started on your journey, or if you are a seasoned follower, to firm up a journey that is well under way. Any growth journey requires steps, and this book is designed to help you learn to take solid steps toward following Christ in a way that will revolutionize how you live. A word of caution: relationships and lives are built over time. Be patient, let Christ lead you in "His way," and give Him the opportunity to mold you into a transformed, fully alive follower.

This particular book aims at giving you "another chance" at getting your "spiritual" life back. In it you will learn Who Jesus is, where He tells us to go to grow in Him, what faith is, how faith develops, how to hear God's voice, and what obedience is. We are not seeking to impress you with biblical insight. We do not seek to wire the entire theological house; instead, we seek to make plain the steps necessary to walk in "His way" in the easiest manner possible.

Instead of placing the bibliography at the back of the book, I thought I would put it at the front. While I do not footnote this book, I could not have written it without the great influence of the following authors:

Connor, Kevin. *The Foundations of Christian Doctrine*. Tonbridge, Kent, England: Sovereign World International and Portland, OR: City Bible Publishing, 1980.

Cordeiro, Wayne. *The Divine Mentor.* Grand Rapids, MI: Bethany House, 2007.

Rainer, Thom S. and Art Rainer. *Simple Life*. Nashville, TN: B&H Publishing Group, 2009.

Smith, Huston,.*The Soul Of Christianity.* San Francisco, CA: Harper Collins, 2005.

Stott, John R.W. *Basic Christianity*. Grand Rapids, MI: Erdmans Pub, 1958.

Stott, John R.W. *The Authority Of The Bible*. Downers Grove, Il: InterVarsity Press, 1974.

Part 1

Why Read the Scriptures?

Ch. 1

God Wants to Be Discovered

The Beginning Days

The day after I gave my life to Christ, I entered a classroom and walked toward a seat. In front of me I saw a student with a book. Moments before the class was to start, I asked him what he was reading. He responded, "The Bible." It was not like any Bible I had ever seen. I was used to a black, leather-bound book that remained sacred and on a shelf for use at church on Sundays only. He handed it to me, and in a few fleeting seconds I simply mumbled, "I wish I had a Bible like this." The bell rang, the class started, and I would never have recalled the event again except for one vital detail. The next day, that same student came in, toting a Bible exactly like the one he had been reading, and gave it to me. Nervously, I thanked him. Starting that day, in that classroom, I devoured the Book day after day for the next six months. I read that Bible until the bindings were busted, every page tattered, every Scripture marked, and the book itself could not possibly handle any further "loving" use. I am often amused that a few seconds of noticing a Bible and the kind heart of a fellow follower changed the course of my entire life.

My Logic Is Not Circular

Some have proposed that we followers of Christ think and believe in a locked box. They say we assume Scripture is inspired because God told us it was; we assume Jesus is the Lord because the Scripture that God told us was inspired tells us who He is. When it comes to my own journey as a follower of Christ, this is not at all how it happened.

Those first days as I pored over the Scripture, I was not thinking, "I am reading an inspired text." In fact, God (to that point) had not told me that what I was reading was inspired, breathed, or spoken by Him. All I knew about the text was that it was compelling, rich, heart-moving, and mind-gripping. I assumed the pages were historical, penned by eyewitnesses who felt and saw something regarding the person of Christ that they believed to be true. The more I read these twenty-seven documents of the New Testament (especially the four Gospel witnesses concerning Christ), something began to happen in my soul: faith was born. What I mean by faith, as I will explain later, is that I came to trust the Christ about who I read in the Scriptures. You might ask, "Didn't you do that when you gave your heart to Christ?" No, not exactly. I was a mess. I needed help. I was coming to Jesus because I did not know where else to go. I was told about Him and His forgiveness, love, mercy, grace, and power. I was told He was Lord, He died and rose again, and He could change my life. I sincerely believed that those who told me about Jesus believed in Him, so I needed to check Him out myself by giving Him my heart. The next day, the journey led me to the Bible. The Bible began to explain exactly Who Jesus is, the promises He had made to me, and the future He had promised. I tested out some of those promises by faith and discovered they were true and reliable. I believed Jesus to be Lord long before I understood what Jesus had to say about Scripture itself.

I did not start with believing the Bible was inspired. I started reading historical documents concerning eyewitness impressions. While reading, I found Christ to be the Son of God, the promised and anointed King, the suffering Servant, and the risen and glorious Son. I discovered that this book called the Bible is not like other books. It possesses a supernatural unity, a revealing of themes unthinkable in other religions and philosophies, an influence that guides the reader away from self and self-improvement, and a disclosed honesty that is not human at all, but God-like. That was a long sentence to simply say that the Bible I was reading was unlike any other sacred text, and to deny that would be to lie to my own heart.

I have never mentally worked in a locked box or system of thought. I read the book many, many times and discovered Jesus, God's Son, revealed in its pages. The Gospel preached in the New Testament led me to a full-on faith in the Son of God based on sound evidence, honest thinking, and (most of all) the compassionate revealing of the Holy Spirit to my soul. One could say the Scriptures led me to Christ, and Christ has led me back to Scripture.

Christ Led Me to Scripture and Scripture Led Me to Christ

Christ originally led me to Scripture as a place to read the documentation about His life, death, resurrection, and ascension. While in Scripture, I found out much more about the One I gave my heart to on a Sunday night back in April of 1972. I gave my heart to a Savior someone claimed could help me. I went to the Scripture and discovered in its books the anointed King (Matthew), the suffering Servant (Mark), the Son of God (Luke), the glorious Lord (John), and the risen Christ (Acts). In reading the Scripture, I found Jesus Christ, to Whom I not only gave my heart, but Whose call I also needed to fully follow.

Christ called me to give Him my heart. I did, and the first place to which I turned was the Scripture. The Scripture revealed Christ to me as the martyred authors of the Bible told me what they had seen, heard, and experienced on their journeys with Christ. They gave particular attention to the irrefutable evidence of His resurrected body.

When introduced to "the Christ" revealed by the Gospel writers, I moved from giving my heart to Christ to becoming His follower. As a follower of Christ, I listened carefully to what Jesus taught and did, especially His clear message that Scripture is God's inspired Word.

Thus, Christ led me to Scripture. In the context of that Scripture, I found material that introduced me to Christ as Lord. That Lord then led me to the whole Bible as the inspired authority for following Him.

The Question that Cannot Be Dodged

No reasonable doubt denies the existence of Jesus. Secular writers and historians have affirmed that He lived, so the question of all questions is not, "Did Jesus live?," but, "Who is Jesus really?"

Those early days when I first began to read Scripture with such zeal, I made so many simple and clearly erroneous assumptions, but I remained blind. I remember, as I read that first Bible, that I sought to discover all I could about God. I sought to understand everything my brain could compute. I asked questions of brilliant people and read deep and mystical books (Watchman Nee was my author of choice). I expended all this effort so I could find God.

Years ago, when I was just a boy, I got myself a bit turned around in the woods on a hunting trip. I was lost and not sure in which direction I should walk. I finally walked out on the crest of a ridge to see if I could gain my bearings by spotting something familiar. I couldn't. I had no clue where to go. Just then, my dad emerged on the next ridge over. I stood up as if I had been hunting game and was not in a desperate search for a familiar landmark. He waved me to come to the ridge on which he was standing some distance away. Gladly, I made my way over. From the moment I saw my dad, I was no longer lost. I knew where I was, but I still needed to search for the best route across the ravine to reach him. While making my way toward him, I constantly searched for the best route. I kept that ridge in sight. I was not lost; I knew where I was. I knew where my dad was, but I was still searching—not to be found, but I was searching to more clearly and closely find my dad.

Wow, was I embarrassed when I discovered that in all my searching for God, I only proved that I was not the one searching for Him as much as I was the one who had been searched for. God came to me and gave me a Bible, then gave me questions to ask, men to mentor me, and books to read. He found me. I have never searched for Him as one who is lost, because when you are spiritually lost you are also deceived. Meaning, you don't know you're lost. You think you know where you are.

Christianity begins with God searching for and coming to us. My searching is mere evidence that God has found me, and now I am following Him out of my lost condition. I thought I was doing all the searching only to discover (long before it occurred to me that I should search) that God came searching for me. I did not find myself in the woods that day; my dad did. I didn't know where I was, but when I caught a glimpse of him, I knew which way to go. If you are interested in reading the Bible and searching for God, be assured that you have already been found. You are not so much searching for God as you are searching for how to fully follow the One who has found you.

How Does God Come to Search for Us?

FIRST, God seeks for us in creation. We have no conscious thought of Him, no longing for Him, no existent thoughts to even care about Him, yet God comes and finds us by creating us from nothing. *"In the beginning God created the heavens and the earth." "Know that the Lord, He is God; it is He Who has made us, and not we ourselves; we are His people and the sheep of His pasture"* (Genesis 1:1; Psalm 100:3 NKJV).

SECOND, God seeks for us in revelation. Again, we are far from God with no ability to conceive Who He really is, but God takes the initiative in revealing Himself to us so we can know Him personally. God is not of this world. God is not made up of the same material we are. Without God's revealing Himself to us, we would never be able to see Him. God would have none of it. He comes searching for us by revealing Himself to us. *"God, Who at various times and in various ways spoke in time past to the fathers by the prophets, has in these last days spoken to us by His Son"* (Hebrews 1:1-2 NKJV).

FINALLY, God seeks for us in the person of His Son Jesus Christ. With our having only a general understanding of God through creation and a moral understanding of Him through His prophets and the writers of the Old Testament, God sent His Son Jesus to search for us. In this way we can know God personally for Who He really is. *"For the Son of Man has come to seek and to save that which was lost"* (Luke 19:10 NKJV). When Jesus shows up, the lights turn on and the "God" of the Old Testament becomes the "Father God" of the New Testament. Jesus shows us the love of God, which the law of God could never unveil. Jesus is the perfect reflection of who God is because Jesus is God Himself. *"This Son perfectly mirrors God, and is stamped with God's nature"* (Hebrews 1:3 MSG).

We Have a Problem

When it comes to knowing and understanding God, we are way out of our depth. We have no instruments to plumb the magnitude of God's metaphysical world. We are completely dependent upon God to reveal Himself to us as He so does in the person of Jesus Christ.

God created, God spoke (through prophets of old), and God lives (in the person of Jesus Christ). We have never sought for Him. He has sought for us, and our seeking of Him is the proof to our hearts that we have been found. Our seeking of Him is not groping around in the dark, but instead seeking where and how He wishes us to follow Him.

He has found us, but it is not easy for us to hear His voice or see His form in order to follow Him perfectly as He leads us through life. Once you are fully convinced that Jesus is Lord, then you will more than gladly embrace His solution to the problem of hearing His voice and seeing His form.

My Faith Rests on These Four Essential Facts about Christ:

The brilliant have debated the question, "Who is Jesus?," for years. Some believe one thing and some another. For me, faith is not blind. It is not an unreasonable leap. It is not, as one great thinker put it, a leap with little knowledge. Faith, for me, is built on the highly combustible evidence that has sparked a wildfire of faith in my heart for over three decades.

FIRST, as we have said, I receive Jesus as the final and most complete search that God has made for humanity and for me in particular. Not the Jesus in heaven with God, but the Jesus on earth doing miracles, teaching the Good News, dying on the cross, rising from the dead, sending people to tell what they had seen. Rather, He is the Jesus ascending to the Father and pouring out His Holy Spirit so that the message could be penned and delivered to the world and, at long last, to me. Jesus is God's greatest evidence for His existence.

How do I know Jesus comes searching? To begin with, Jesus' existence is undeniable. Not even a reliable, secular source would deny His existence. Second, no reliable source of material anywhere would indicate that Jesus came and did anything but search for lost people, saving them from blindness, bondage, oppression, aimlessness, fear, and everything else of harm. He is declared by all evidence to be without defect—kind and compassionate. *"The Spirit of the Lord is upon me, because He has anointed me to preach the gospel to the poor; He has sent me to heal the brokenhearted, to proclaim liberty to the captives and recovery of sight to the blind, to set at liberty those who are oppressed; to proclaim the acceptable year of the Lord"* (Luke 4:18-19 NKJV).

SECOND, I remember the claims of Christ. All other religious teachers direct people to the truth they teach. I am a teacher of the Gospel. I do not direct people to myself for help, but to the truth where the real help exists: Jesus. In every religion, teachers direct followers to the truth and only indirectly to themselves. At best, the great masters of religion only point to themselves as having discovered the secret truth and passing it on. Muhammad points to his Qur'an, Buddha points to his "Noble Path," Krishna points to his philosophies, and Zoroaster points to his ethics; in each case they are separate from their teaching—unlike Christ and His claims.

No reasonable, sane teacher ever claimed to be the truth. They all claimed to know the truth and to be revealing the truth. Jesus is the exception. He declares Himself to *be* "the Truth." Either He is correct and He is "the Truth," or He is insane. I vote for "the Truth." Any other explanation leads to complete absurdity and lack of honesty.

And Jesus said to them, "I am the bread of life." John 6:35 NKJV

Then Jesus spoke to them again, saying, "I am the light of the world." John 8:12 NKJV

Jesus said to them, "Most assuredly, I say to you, before Abraham was, I AM." John 8:58 NKJV

"I am the good shepherd. The good shepherd gives His life for the sheep." John 10:11 NKJV

Jesus said to her, "I am the resurrection and the life. He who believes in Me, though he may die, he shall live." John 11:25 NKJV

Jesus said to him, "I am the way, the truth, and the life. No one comes to the Father except through Me." John 14:6 NKJV

"Come to Me, all you who labor and are heavy laden, and I will give you rest." Matthew 11:28 NKJV

It is not merely unusual for a teacher to make claims like these; it has, in fact, never been done. No teacher has been able to make such claims and back them up with evidence as Jesus did.

THIRD, I look to the character of Christ. He is without sin, and His character is flawless; we know this on many levels.

What Does Jesus Think about Himself?

Jesus is aware that He is without sin. He is the Shepherd doing the searching; He is the light to those in darkness. He is truth to those deceived. He is bread to the hungry, and He is the one calling sinners to come unto Himself. What person have you ever known who challenged his or her enemies to try to find sin in them? And yet Jesus does. *"Which of you convicts Me of sin?"* (John 8:46 NKJV) Jesus viewed Himself as a sinless being, searching for sin-infected people.

What His Legalistic, Familiar Disciples Think of Jesus

Peter declares, after spending hours with Jesus, that He is *"… a lamb without blemish and without spot,"* *"Who committed no sin, nor was deceit found in His mouth; Who, when He was reviled, did not revile in return; when He suffered, He did not threaten, but committed Himself to Him who judges righteously"* (1 Peter 1:19; 2:22-23 NKJV). After Jesus dies, Peter has ample opportunity to say, "By the way, this one time I caught Jesus being selfish toward me," but he doesn't. Not even once. Not one disciple does, including his betrayer.

John is a sensitive guy who declares this about Jesus: *"And you know that He was manifested to take away our sins, and in Him there is no sin"* (1 John 3:5 NKJV).

Everyone knows how scandal works. If there had been some small sin, it would have hit the presses and been boldly broadcast. However, not even a hint of impropriety is mentioned about Jesus and his relationship with those who follow Him, including the women. His disciples affirm Jesus to be without sin.

What Jesus' Enemies Think of Him

Jesus has five basic accusations leveled against Him:

- He blasphemes because He forgives sin that only God could forgive.
- He associates with evil people.
- He is "Jewish-ly" undisciplined.
- He breaks the Sabbath.
- He makes terrorist-like threats.

Regarding the first accusation, if Jesus is who He claimed to be—"God"—He has every right to forgive sin. Regarding the second accusation, He is full of grace and indeed is a "friend of sinners," yet He is also separate from sinners (*"who is holy, harmless, undefiled, separate from sinners"* Hebrews 7:26 NKJV). Regarding the third accusation, no one can ever doubt His commitment to His cause. Whether He fasts enough or not is much less compelling than the fact that Jesus "fasts" His life on the cross to prove His level of commitment to the Jewish faith by dying for all their sins. Regarding the fourth accusation, if He is the Lord of the Sabbath, He has a right to set aside the traditions the religious leaders add to the Scriptures regarding Sabbath practice (Mark 2:28). In regard to the fifth accusation, He is clear that He is talking about the Temple of God (His own body), not their Temple (Matthew 26:61). If He is God, however, would He not have a right to tear down His temple and build a new one, especially if the replacement turn-around was only three days?

Beyond the unsubstantiated accusations of the religious leaders, Pontius Pilate declares himself to be "innocent of this man's blood" (Matthew 27:24 NLT). Herod could find no fault in Jesus (Luke 23:4). Even Judas, who had betrayed Him, declares Him to be innocent (Matthew 27:3-4).

Jesus' character is flawless. He stands as the only man in history against whom no sin can be leveled and sustained; His enemies try and are all overthrown. The only ones that dig up "sin" on Christ are His haters. They do not come at the subject with great objectivity and are overthrown as bad liars.

FOURTH, I think of the resurrection of Jesus. The tomb is empty. The grave clothes remain behind and untouched (save the face cloth). Countless witnesses see Jesus and are martyred, bearing witness to the truth of what they had seen. This is all compelling evidence not only that Jesus lived, which is without debate, but also that He rose from the dead. To add a bit of insult to injury toward those so determined to refute the resurrection of Christ, you also have the radical character transformation in the cowardly disciples who witnessed it. This final piece of evidence puts the finishing touches on the proof of Who Christ is. If Jesus is risen from the dead, then He truly is the Lord and Christ of all (Acts 4:10-12), and we will want to listen to what He has to say about authority and Scripture.

Ch. 2

A Reliable Absolute

The Authority of Scripture

When I first read the Bible back in 1972, the Vietnam War was coming to an end. Watergate was surfacing with the sexual revolution in full bloom, free thought abounded, social and ethical permissiveness raved rampant, and a unifying revolt against authority manifested itself on college campuses. The debate developing then, which has now turned atomic, is simple to define: are truth and righteousness relative or absolute?

If truth is "relative," it is because there is no God Who, by revelation, has shown us His standards for right and wrong. Instead of truth being absolute, it can be personal: "What is truth for me may not be truth for you."

If truth is absolute, then there is a God Who has revealed His truth. We are called upon to hear His truth, agree with His truth, and obey His truth. Truth is not personal and does not belong to us, but to God. It is God's truth and not truth that we can make up for ourselves.

In those early days of Bible reading, I can remember thinking that I was in an all-out pursuit of God. I was going to find Him, comprehend Him, pin Him down, and make Him understandable to others. I would never have assumed back then that if I could have comprehended Him, I would never have really known Him. For, if I could have comprehended an infinite God with my finite mind, then the God I comprehended could never be God at all.

Truth is also that way; it is infinite. We do not find God or truth; God finds us and reveals Himself to us in ways we can only partially understand. Our searching is not the search to find something lost, but the search to understand Who has found us.

Jesus found me. I read Scripture. I discovered Jesus was fully God and was calling me to follow Him fully. As I began to follow Him, I started realizing that He wanted to lead me through Scripture. I discovered Christ and His Scripture to be the source of God's authority for guiding my life and practice.

Jesus on the Old Testament Scripture

When it comes to the origin of Jesus' teaching, He makes it clear that He teaches what the Father tells Him to teach.

> *"All things have been delivered to Me by My Father, and no one knows the Son except the Father."* Matthew 11:27 NKJV

> *Jesus answered them and said, "My doctrine is not Mine, but His who sent Me."* John 7:16 NKJV

How does the Father give Jesus His doctrine and deliver "all things" to Him? We know for certain that Jesus prays, and His Father does reveal things to Him, but more than that, we discover that Jesus appeals to Scripture.

He Respects the Accuracy and Power of Old Testament Scripture

"Do not think that I came to destroy the Law or the Prophets. I did not come to destroy but to fulfill." Matthew 5:17 NKJV

He Respects the Authority of Old Testament Scripture

Whomever you give permission to tell you "no" establishes their authority over you. Jesus allows Scripture to say "no" to His life, particularly in regard to His temptation encounter.

"It is written, 'Man shall not live by bread alone, but by every word that proceeds from the mouth of God.'" Matthew 4:4 NKJV

"It is written again, 'You shall not tempt the Lord your God.'" Matthew 4:7 NKJV

"Away with you, Satan! For it is written, 'You shall worship the Lord your God, and Him only you shall serve.'" Matthew 4:10 NKJV

The small phrase "it is written" is plenty to satisfy Jesus in determining God's will and ways.

He Respects the Declared Destiny of Old Testament Scripture

Without question, Jesus reads the Old Testament passages that vividly describe who He is: the promised King, the suffering Servant, the Son of God, and the risen Lord. He synthesizes all of this together and knows that He, as God's Son, must submit to what God wants fulfilled. Listen to what Jesus tells Peter on the night of His betrayal:

"Put away your sword," Jesus told him. "Those who use the sword will die by the sword. Don't you realize that I could ask My Father for thousands of angels to protect us, and He would send them instantly? But if I did, how would the Scriptures be fulfilled that describe what must happen now?" Matthew 26:52-54 NLT

Regarding everything that is happening to Him, Jesus says, *"But this is all happening to fulfill the words of the prophets as recorded in the Scriptures"* (Matthew 26:56 NLT). Jesus reads the Scriptures and knows what they say regarding His life. They become a source of direction and destiny for Him (Mark 9:12).

He Respects Old Testament Scripture as a Source to Settle Disputes

When people come asking questions, Jesus directs them back to Scripture by asking, "What does the Scripture say?" When the rich young ruler wants to know how to inherit eternal life, when the scribes want to know how marriage worked in heaven, when teaching the Sermon on the Mount, Jesus appeals and builds on the Old Testament as His authoritative base (Luke 10:25-26; Mark 12:18-27; Matthew 5-7).

Over and over again, Jesus appeals to the Old Testament as God's authority on a matter. When challenged on cleaning up the temple by driving out the marketers, Jesus appeals to Old Testament Scripture as the foundation for His authority for action (Mark 11:15-18). When He engages in healing people, He backs His action up with Scripture from the Old Testament (Luke 14:1-6). Even in overturning traditions that religious leaders have added to God's Word, Jesus appeals to Scripture for a clearer understanding and a foundation for His authority. Over and over again, Jesus appeals to the Old Testament for His authority for action (Matthew 12:1-7).

He Respects Old Testament Scripture as Written By Prophets Sent to Reveal God's Word

When God calls a prophet or a servant to deliver a message, He often uses the word "send." He makes it clear that He is sending them to deliver His message.

"Come now, therefore, and I will send you to Pharaoh that you may bring My people, the children of Israel, out of Egypt."
Exodus 3:10 NKJV

Also I heard the voice of the Lord, saying, "Whom shall I send, and who will go for Us?" Then I said, "Here am I! Send me." And He said, "Go, and tell this people…." Isaiah 6:8-9 NKJV

But the Lord said to me, "Do not say, 'I am a youth,' for you shall go to all to whom I send you, and whatever I command you, you shall speak."
Jeremiah 1:7 NKJV

And He said to me, "Son of man, I am sending you to the children of Israel…." Ezekiel 2:3 NKJV

These were the prophets of old, sent to speak and reveal God's word and message.

Jesus Names Them "Apostles"

The word "apostle" in the New Testament means to send as an ambassador or (as I like to put it) to send someone to carry a message from another. One day, a friend of mine was reading a paper and noticed that they were looking for "apostles." He chuckled, because the paper was a Greek paper in which some company was looking for a bike courier and used a form of this Greek word "apostle" to advertise for a job. A New Testament "apostle" was a sort of mail courier for God; he delivered the message God was sending.

Just as God chose to send prophets in the Old Testament to declare His message, Jesus chooses to send out "apostles" to declare His Good News. Notice that Jesus chooses them from among His disciples. He chooses twelve, names them "apostles," and calls them to be with Him that He might send them out with His message (Mark 3:14). All of Jesus' language and action are setting the stage for Scripture to be written.

In the course of time, three other apostles are named to this list: James (the brother of Jesus), who becomes the pastor of the Jerusalem church (Galatians 1:19); Paul, who is converted on the road to Damascus (Acts 26:17; Galatians 1:1); and Matthias, who takes Judas's place (Acts 1:16-26). Other apostles are mentioned in Scripture, but these designated "apostles" of Christ are few and special. Why?

An "apostle" is someone sent by Jesus, in His authority, to represent Him and to teach in His name. These apostles are so identified with Jesus that He declares that any who receive them are receiving Jesus Himself (Matthew 10:40-42; John 13:20).

From the beginning, the church has been devoting itself to what the apostles are saying. The members understand that a special inspiration is upon them to explain what they have witnessed, as well as the Good News of the Kingdom of God that Jesus has taught them. These men are special gifts to the church, and they have power as they teach God's Word to equip people to fully follow Christ (Ephesians 4:11-19).

Jesus Promises Holy Spirit Help to Write Scriptures

As Jesus is preparing to leave the earth, He gathers His apostles together and promises help to send to enable them to succeed in their calling.

> *"These things I have spoken to you while being present with you. But the Helper, the Holy Spirit, whom the Father will send in My name, He will teach you all things, and bring to your remembrance all things that I said to you."* John 14:25-26 NKJV

The Holy Spirit is going to be sent with a huge task. He is going to make them remember teachings they otherwise would have forgotten, not understanding the importance and relevance when Jesus said them. The Holy Spirit is going to refresh their memories so that they will be able to write the Gospels.

The apostles could not comprehend everything while Jesus was with them, so Jesus promises to send them the Holy Spirit to guide them into a truth they have never heard before.

> *"I still have many things to say to you, but you cannot bear them now. However, when He, the Spirit of truth, has come, He will guide you into all truth; for He will not speak on His own authority, but whatever He hears He will speak; and He will tell you things to come."*
> John 16:12-13 NKJV

By the Holy Spirit's guiding the disciples into a truth they have not heard before, Jesus is making provision for them to write the Epistles. In this way, everything God needed to tell us would be in place, written in both the Gospels and the Epistles.

Hence, Jesus sent the Holy Spirit to the apostles so they could write Scripture.

The Apostles Order Their Writings to Be Read

As these New Testament Scriptures are being written, the "apostles" order them to be read publicly along with the Old Testament Scriptures (Colossians 4:16; 1 Thessalonians 5:27; Revelations 1:3), a tradition that was practiced for centuries in theChurch.

The church recognizes and proclaims that it is built on the foundation of the "apostles" (those sent with God's inspired message), with Jesus as its cornerstone. To be built on the foundation of the apostles means that it is built on the "message" or "Scripture" the apostles spoke and wrote (Ephesians 2:19-20).

Paul Declares the Written Works of the Apostles to Be Inspired

Toward the end of Paul's journey, after much of the New Testament Scriptures have circulated, Paul writes and tells his son Timothy, *"All*

Scripture is given by inspiration of God, and is profitable for doctrine, for re-proof, for correction, for instruction in righteousness, that the man of God may be complete, thoroughly equipped for every good work" (2 Timothy 3:16-17 NKJV). It is clear to Paul that the message the apostles had been faithful in preaching possesses the authority to transform the life and heart of a person who, by faith, follows Christ.

With all the debate over relative and absolute authority, Jesus should get the final say. He is, without debate, the Son of God. He set an example of appealing to Scripture as His authority. He provided for New Testament Scripture to be written. How can we deny Him?

Christ as the head of His Church and the Scripture as His Words become, to me as a follower, my authority and the standard of my practice, but not in a legal sense or in a read-and-do obligation. The Scripture becomes the place where Christ reveals Himself and expounds to me His will over a lifetime of searching to follow Him. The longer I follow, the longer I search for Him in the passages, the more clearly His ways become known to me, but especially, the more clearly I see Him and He is seen in me.

If Jesus uses Scripture as a source for His authority and for relationship building with the Father, could we consider doing anything less?

Putting It All in Perspective

The goal of the book you now hold is to help followers deepen their faith and relationship with Christ through Bible reading. Your question may be, "Why so much time talking about Jesus and who He is?" Let me make it clear. I do not, nor do I encourage you, to read your Bible because it is an interesting book, or more sacred than all others, or because it has better stories, will make you wise, or is the most popular and well-quoted book ever written. I do not encourage you to read it daily because of its unity, its themes, its amazing history and preservation, or because it is unlike any other book with its stark honesty. I encourage you to read it because Christ so honored it, so provided for its writing, and as the undisputed Lord, has commissioned us to listen to His Word and therein to find a source of faith that unlocks God's cascading and immeasurable grace.

When my father passed on a few years ago, something other than his physical body left me on the day of his death. It was the sense of someone pulling for me. When I entered this world, my parents, more than all others, wanted me to succeed. They believed in me, protected me, and looked upon me like no one else could or can. The day after my dad went to be with Jesus, I deeply felt that void. Then I remembered, as much as my parents loved me, their love could not equate to God's love in Christ for me. I don't read the Bible because some bullying God wishes to push me around with His unreasonable demands. I read the Bible because the Father in heaven desperately wants me to succeed and desperately wants to reveal Himself to me so I can know Him and thus know myself.

I read because the Lord Jesus has asked it of me. I keep my motivation to read because, within the margins of the pages, I discover a God Who would literally rather die than see me fail.

Part 2

How Should I Read Scripture?

Ch. 3

RPMs–Reading

Faith relationship is built as we listen to God's voice (Romans 10:14), and His voice is best heard as we devote ourselves to habitual and consistent daily reading of Scripture. Faith does not accidentally appear; rather, it is a consequence of hearing God speak (Romans 10:17). If I read God's Word and seek to listen to God's voice, I become a self-feeder (one who is taking appropriate responsibility in his walk and relationship with Christ).

God gives us no form to follow in regard to reading His Word. We only know two things about the early church: they gave their attention to God's Word daily, and they listened to His Word together (*"And they continued steadfastly in the apostles' doctrine and fellowship, in the breaking of bread, and in prayers"* Acts 2:42 NKJV). We use a basic pattern for our time with Jesus that we call "RPMs." RPMs form an acrostic that helps us remember how to get the most out of our Bible reading.

Read Pray Meditate Sign

As I noted in the preface to this book, revolutions create energy and movement. Let me take a moment to break down the original acrostic, "Revolutions Per Minute." When you read the Word, you allow your life to revolve and rotate around Christ and His will. You remove worldly lust as the axle of your life, and you put Christ and His Word at the center.

"Per" is the multiplying factor. When you add prayer to reading, it moves eternity into time and space. It brings the presence of God to earth. When God is present, so is His power.

"Minute" is how the revolutions are measured. Once you begin meditating on God's Word (and more specifically on what God is saying to you), then heaven touches earth, spirit touches matter, and God touches your heart in time and space through meditation.

Lastly, the "S" is merely the suffix that makes the acrostic plural. When you sign Jesus' name to a prayer, an insight, or a prompting from God, it's like God signs your name to the request. It's plural because both Christ and you are deeply involved.

Why have a process like RPMs to read through the Bible with others? Our Devotional Experience (yearly reading guide) and RPMs enable you to read Scriptures with others who share your desire to grow in faith. RPMs gives you the ability to compare insights and ask questions with those who are reading the same narratives. RPMs slows you down so you can really listen. Lastly, RPMs can hold you accountable as you daily chart your journey.

One day, a woman was trying to balance her checkbook to no avail. She was a few dollars off, and there was no possible reconciliation in sight. Finally, she bowed her head and asked God for help. She then fervently continued the search, but met no success. With disgust, she got up to fetch a drink of water. About halfway through the glass, while she was thinking about what to make for dinner, she remembered something she had neglected to check. Within moments, her checkbook was reconciled. God speaks through our thoughts even when we are consciously thinking about other things. We read Scripture in the morning, jot down a few notes, and then give the Holy Spirit the rest of our day to show us things we had never mused about before.

We begin listening to God by reading. Try not to read too much during your reading time so you can reflect and talk to God about what you are reading. Give Him ample time to enlighten your mind. Limit your daily journey to one chapter. As you begin, try to enter the narrative. Entering the narrative means that you read slowly and begin seeking a mental picture of the action in your mind. Depending on the genre or kind of literature you are reading, this might be easy or difficult. To gain the most understanding, try to put what is being said in context with the chapter before. How does what you are reading resolve what came right before?

The Phrase That Captures Your Notice

After you have read the entire chapter, allow a particular verse or phrase to grab your attention or stand out to your heart (Usually this happens through a sense of curiosity: "I wonder what that means," or "I am unusually drawn to that phrase."). You may need to read it two or three times for it to really sink in. Once you clarify the verse or phrase that touches your heart, highlight it or underline it, making it stand out in the text of Scripture. Do something in your Bible that tells you, "I was here, right here with God, and He brought this particular passage to my attention," and then write it down. If you read a chapter and nothing stands out, ask for God's help. Ask Him to guide your mind to a verse or phrase that He wants to highlight in your spirit. It has been my experience that when I read in a determined manner, asking for the Holy Spirit's help,

God responds and something will stand out even in the oddest and least likely passages.

The Big Question

Next, inquire: "What question is the author seeking to answer in the immediate surrounding subject matter that is standing out in my mind?" Spend just a few moments and think about the verse, what question is being answered, and what problem is being resolved. The interrogatives are a great help in forming your questions of the text (who, what, why, when, where, how).

The Bigger Question

Some days you might feel like really stretching and forming a question for an entire event. What question is the author seeking to answer in the entire story? For example, when you read Matthew 4 (regarding the temptation of Jesus), what kind of questions is the author seeking to answer as he tells the story? You might say the author is answering the question of how Jesus fought off temptation. You might say that he is answering the question of how Jesus depended upon the Word of God to battle temptation. You might say the author is answering the question, "Just how determined was the devil to control Jesus?" I realize that usually you ask the question and then give an answer. When it comes to the Word, however, God is giving you an answer. To help our search for Him, He wishes us to formulate the question.

There could be a number of ways to define the question the author is seeking to answer, but be certain of this: the author is always answering a question because the ultimate Author of the Bible is the Holy Spirit. The Holy Spirit provides the answer to all we need answered; our venture is to seek to define the question or questions the author is answering. If you do define the question, you will be reading the Bible with understanding.

The Bigger Yet Question

You might get really bold and define a question that is being answered by the whole chapter you are reading. Let's go back to Matthew 4. You might say the author is answering the question, "How did Jesus launch His ministry in a God-approving way?" You could even put the question another way: "Before Jesus preached the Gospel and a multitude began to follow Him, how did His Father prepare Him for success?"

Once you define the question the passage is answering, you are reading with understanding. To read it any other way causes you to miss so much. The Bible is not a novel or a piece of human literature. It is God's Word, and God is seeking to reveal Himself to you through it. He is seeking to give you answers about Himself that you cannot receive through your senses. Maybe you have seen those large commentaries sitting on a pastor's bookshelf. More likely you may be aware that he possesses gigabytes worth of books by theologians on his computer that are full of answers to questions those theologians asked the Bible. Theologians are not to be the only guys getting in on the fun of learning what God is saying; the Bible was written for all who would follow Jesus. Don't let the journey intimidate you, for you were created to listen to God and get to know Him deeply, as you search Him out through His Word with the Holy Spirit's help.

What about the Wrong Question

You might wonder, "What if I pose a question the author is not answering?" You just might do that, but remember you are going to spend the rest of your life reading this eternal book. It will become a source of faith for you. Each time you read it, your questions will become more accurate because God is going to reveal Himself little by little, thought by thought. That is how He begins with us so we won't ultimately miss the important things, even if at first a thing or two skip our notice. *"He tells us everything over and over—one line at a time, one line at a time, a little here and a little there"* (Isaiah 28:10 NLT). When you first learned to walk, you were a bit wobbly. When you begin reading God's Word, it won't all be comfortable. The longer you hang in there, you are going to have a blast, and your wobbly reading will become confident.

Don't worry about perfection. This is not mechanical; it is relational. God will guide you through your trial and error, and you will be shocked. Even when you are not seeing as clearly as He wants you to, He will use what you are reading to speak to you, build your faith, and transform your life.

Trouble-Shooting

When concentration is lacking, read out loud or read from other translations. If a particular passage is hard to comprehend, pick up another translation and read from it. Sometimes that will break the log-jam. Whatever you do, try not to leave the chapter until you have a phrase that stands out to you and a question that you think the author might be answering.

Summary

- Read a chapter of the Bible.
- Find a phrase or verse that jumps out at your heart.
- Underline, highlight, make what God shows you stand out.
- Ask a question the author is answering.
- While doing this, ask for God's help.

Scripture

Till I come, give attention to reading, to exhortation, to doctrine.
1 Timothy 4:13 NKJV

I charge you by the Lord that this epistle be read to all the holy brethren. 1 Thessalonians 5:25 NKJV

Now when this epistle is read among you, see that it is read also in the church of the Laodiceans, and that you likewise read the epistle from Laodicea. Colossians 4:16 NKJV

Search from the book of the Lord, and read. Isaiah 34:16 NKJV

And it shall be with him, and he shall read it all the days of his life, that he may learn to fear the Lord his God and be careful to observe all the words of this law and these statutes…. Deuteronomy 17:19 NKJV

There was not a word of all that Moses had commanded which Joshua did not read before all the assembly of Israel. Joshua 8:34 NKJV

Ch. 4

RPMs–Prayer

I have discovered that it is essential to pray after reading a Bible chapter. I have tried praying before reading the Bible, only to discover that my spirit is not as tuned to God as it is after I read. I have tried praying after meditation, only to discover that prayer beforehand paves the way for great communion with God. Prayer right after reading my chapter, right after defining the question the author is asking, right after finding the verse or passage that really jumps out, seems to enrich my encounter the best.

I am often asked, "How long should I pray?" I have discovered that the entire RPMs experience takes me about thirty to forty minutes. Everyone is different. Find your own pace and rhythm with the Lord. I have found that the prayer portion of my Devotional Experience lasts about ten minutes. Obviously, that doesn't mean that this is the only time I pray during RPMs, but it is where my prayer is concentrated in a special way.

Let me give you an example. A young woman married a man from another country. He spoke English, but she did not speak his native language. This went on for about two years, after which she enrolled in an intensive language course in his native tongue. Four years later, she had mastered the language. One day, a friend commented on how kind she was to learn his language so that she could speak to him. She immediately responded that she did not learn his language so she could speak better to him. He heard and understood her with ease. She learned his language for the same reason we learn to pray—so she could hear the depths of his heart as he spoke to her in his language.

Jesus' disciples wanted to learn how to pray, so Jesus taught them. In the prayer Jesus used as an outline, Jesus gave His disciples five basic topics to pray through. When I pray using these five topics, I am certain I am praying about that which is in line with His will. This prayer was not given to recite; it was given so I would know how to talk to God in a way that would be relationship-building and make me most sensitive to hear His voice.

Jesus' prayer started with adoration, moved to invitation, erupted into dependence, formed contrition in the heart, and concluded with spiritual warfare.

It has been my experience that this prayer is the language God speaks. When we pray His prayer, we pray in a language that God and I can understand. It's God's language because I can pray His will in a way God hears, for He is ever sensitive when He hears a follower praying according to His purposes. It is my language because it allows God to speak back to me in a way I can comprehend.

The Lord's Prayer is a prayer of the heart. Jesus teaches us to pray what is in His heart and what is in our hearts. I might not know it, but God is asking me to pray for that which matters most to Him and to me. It's the perfect prayer that fills both our hearts.

After you have read the "Devotional Experience" chapter, take a few moments to pray, and if you don't know where to start, use the "Jesus Prayer" as an outline. In prayer, we focus our minds and hearts completely on Christ, allowing Him to activate our spirits in ways that only He can.

The Prayer

> 1) *"Our Father in heaven, may Your name be kept holy. 2) May Your Kingdom come soon. May Your will be done on earth, as it is in heaven. 3) Give us today the food we need, 4) and forgive us our sins, as we have forgiven those who sin against us. 5) And don't let us yield to temptation, but rescue us from the evil one."*
> Matthew 6:9-13 NLT [numbering mine]

Adoration

First, I am instructed to come to God as "our Father." He is not merely God, but He is my "Abba" Father, which affectionately means "Daddy" (Romans 8:15). Prayer begins with full confidence that "my Father" is worthy of being trusted as a parent Who cares for me as His child. I am not alone in the world. I have an ever-present Father walking with me and brothers and sisters praying with me. This prayer screams to my heart that God wants a relationship with me, and He wants me to relate to Him as a son would a loving father.

Further, I am to let His name, "Jehovah" or "Yahweh," be set apart from all other names. "Yahweh" means that God will be everything. He is above all else. He is the exclusive God of my heart. He is the "I AM," the source of all that I need. He alone is God. He alone completes and comforts me.

Lastly, when we declare God's name "holy" we recognize that prayer is taking a place of awe. When I talk with God, it is not like talking to someone else. There is an awe in my heart and voice. Yes, God is my friend, but first He is my Father of Whom I am in awe. Prayer begins by bringing God close—"our Father"—and then establishing His distance and greatness—"in heaven." Only when we worship God for His closeness and reflect upon His distance can we genuinely draw near.

Invitation

God's kingdom is God's will, purpose, goals, and objectives. Right from the beginning of my day, I am reminded that I cannot make God's will happen. My best efforts cannot produce God's purposes; only He can. I am called to invite Him to my earth, my world, my circumstances, and my day. When I pray, "Your Kingdom come," I am asking God to transform the world (especially my world) into a place where God reigns, where His standards and values become the governing influences upon my life and upon the world around me.

When I pray "Your kingdom come," I am declaring that God's will and purpose are not visible and do not originate on the earth. They are transcendent from above, greater than my desires and greater than me. When I say "on earth as it is in heaven," I am acknowledging that His invisible will can become visible in my life as He brings it into my heart.

Dependence

Just so I would never think that I am capable of providing for myself, I am encouraged to ask for enough provision today to supply what I need for tomorrow. When tomorrow comes, I am ready to receive again the manna God provides for that day. It is God Who gives wisdom and strength to gain wealth, and it is His blessing of the earth that allows wealth to be accumulated (Deuteronomy 8:18). Thus, I am encouraged daily to take the posture of dependence and let my supply come through God's power.

I am not alone in this; I am bound together with all God's children to receive what is necessary to get me through today and into tomorrow. The fact is, we all receive together what is necessary for all of us to get to tomorrow. So right here in the prayer, I become sensitive with what God has provided for me today that He may lead me to share with others. In this way, all of us together can have our daily needs met. *"Give us this day…."*

God is intent on making sure that, no matter how much provision I think I have stored up, it is God Who sustains me every day. When I pray "give us day by day," I am confessing that God's hands are necessary for my survival. When I pray "our daily bread," I am implying that my hands are necessary to reach out and receive the Lord's provision for that day. I need the strength of God's hand for the provision. I need strength in my hand to receive so that I am not tempted to take things by my own strength (and burden my life with residual debt).

Contrition

My sin separates me from God, just like it does from any other relationship. If I offend a friend, it immediately changes our relationship. It is exactly the same way with God, for different reasons. When I sin, God still loves me, but my relationship changes. God is not so much unable to be around me when I sin; it is my guilt and poor self-image that make it impossible for me to be confident around Him.

He cured all my sin messes through Jesus' death on the cross. He forgives everyone in the same way. For me to experience this forgiveness, however, I must genuinely receive it with a grateful heart. Some may offend me with an offense so serious that I do not warrant them worthy of forgiveness. However, I then remember that my self-centered, hard heart also made my offense serious to God, yet His love drove Him to forgive me.

God gives me a special gift: I can measure the depth of my hardness of heart toward God by asking the question, "Against whom do I still hold an offense?" In this prayer, Jesus aims right to the root of my heart, for only a contrite, broken, tender heart admits sin and receives forgiveness. Only tender, broken hearts forgive those who have sinned against them. If I am offended at someone, I am not yet tender toward God; if I forgive another, my heart is soft enough to receive His forgiveness. This prayer keeps us from becoming hard-hearted and miserable with the poison of bitterness.

When I pray the Lord's prayer, I receive forgiveness. I am then able to give forgiveness to others, keeping peace among God, my heart, and others. Daily I remember I have sinned; daily I am reminded to let it go and to forgive others, the same way Jesus forgave me. "God in Christ forgiving" (Ephesians 4:32).

Spiritual Warfare

Every day while in prayer, I remind myself that I need God's help to keep me from yielding to temptation. I know from experience that if I yield, I will soon be addicted. Here I can call out to Christ on both accounts, "Keep me from lust, and where lust owns me by way of addiction, deliver me out of it." This is the very heart of our warfare against the enemy—depending on Christ to keep us from and to get us out of it. The book of James says that I am tempted when my lust is enticed by something. How do you build lust? Lust is built by thinking about something long enough until it pushes past your emotion right into a desire: "I want." The Lord's Prayer keeps our desires in check by focusing our thoughts on Him.

This prayer captures the voice of the faithful: "Don't lead me over there to what I cannot see, and deliver me out of this evil right now that I do see." It covers both our areas of concern: temptations we cannot see (or know that are coming) and the evil present within us from which we must be delivered.

This prayer is an important moment in our daily time with God, for it moves us from the cerebral into the transcendental. The Lord's Prayer activates resident faith and places our focus on God. Prayer tells our brain that we are more interested in what God has to say about the text we are reading and less interested in our own crafty insight.

The Lord's Prayer cleans our needs and concerns. We need a relationship with God "our Father." We need a divine purpose, "Your kingdom come." We need daily provision, "our daily bread." We need continual restoration, "forgive us." And we need to be kept from fatal lusts and destructive addictions, "lead us not into temptation." This prayer is written in our language, for it deals with every one of our most essential needs. Also, it is written in God's language, for it reveals God's greatest desire and purpose toward us.

What about Prayers That God Does Not Answer?

We will never know why some prayers go unanswered. People have written many books on the subject, and most of them end up revealing to me that I have prayed wrongly. By the time I work out all the things I have done wrong in prayer, I have lost interest in praying altogether. My approach is a bit different. I am interested in what is going on when I pray, not in what isn't. The temptation is to focus on what is not being answered or listened to, instead of what God has promised to do when I pray. One thing we know for sure is that God's presence is always manifest when people have been praying over a prolonged period of time. So, between the prayers being prayed, during the time period and just before, God manifests Himself in what is going on. To say it another way, I experience pain and begin to pray for its removal, and I pray over a long time period. During that time, before the pain departs, what is God doing when He is not removing the pain? By way of insight, notice that in the Lord's prayer we are never called upon to pray for the removal of pain.

To learn what happens, let me take you through the whole context of the Lord's prayer in Luke. I realize the passage is long, but we must hear God's whole teaching on prayer to fully understand what He was teaching His disciples about it.

> *Now it came to pass, as He was praying in a certain place, when He*
> *ceased, that one of His disciples said to Him, "Lord, teach us to pray,*
> *as John also taught his disciples."*
> *So He said to them, "When you pray, say:*
> *'Our Father in heaven, Hallowed be Your name.*
> *Your Kingdom come.*
> *Your will be done on earth as it is in heaven.*
> *Give us day by day our daily bread.*
> *And forgive us our sins,*
> *for we also forgive everyone who is indebted to us.*
> *And do not lead us into temptation, but deliver us from the evil one.'"*
> Luke 11:1-4 NKJV

Here, as we have shown, Jesus was teaching His disciples what to say in prayer. Now He is going to teach them "how" to pray by using a common story about a friend in need at midnight.

And He said to them, "Which of you shall have a friend, and go to him at midnight and say to him, 'Friend, lend me three loaves; for a friend of mine has come to me on his journey, and I have nothing to set before him'; and he will answer from within and say, 'Do not trouble me; the door is now shut, and my children are with me in bed; I cannot rise and give to you'? I say to you, though he will not rise and give to him because he is his friend, yet because of his persistence he will rise and give him as many as he needs." Luke 11:5-8 NKJV

The point of the story is obvious. A grumpy friend at midnight, who is snug in bed with his house all locked up, outer gate and all, is reluctant to get up and meet a need. If the friend in need stays persistent, however, the grumpy friend will rise and give him what he wants just to rid himself of the nuisance. Jesus contrasts the grumpy friend with God, and there is no contest. God does not slumber nor sleep, so persistence with Him will have a very different effect and outcome. Jesus now moves from "how" to pray (with persistence) to the "promise" of persistent prayer.

"So I say to you, ask, and it will be given to you; seek, and you will find; knock, and it will be opened to you. For everyone who asks receives, and he who seeks finds, and to him who knocks it will be opened."
Matthew 7:7,8 NKJV

The promise of persistent praying is receiving, finding, having things opened. This is the motivation for being persistent; not because God is reluctant to give, but because He has so much He wishes to lavish upon our lives. God seeks for persistence in prayer because there is so much to give.

The teaching is over, right? Actually, not quite, because Christ wants to teach us what we will receive every time we pray.

"If a son asks for bread from any father among you, will he give him a stone? Or if he asks for a fish, will he give him a serpent instead of a fish? Or if he asks for an egg, will he offer him a scorpion? If you then,

being evil, know how to give good gifts to your children, how much more will your heavenly Father give the Holy Spirit to those who ask Him!" Luke 11:9-14 NKJV

We do not know if God will remove the pain or the difficulty from our present circumstance, but we do know that every time we pray we will receive the Holy Spirit. The Holy Spirit is the greatest of all gifts, for He will work inside our lives to make our external burdens easy-lifting. The Holy Spirit is the greatest gift you can receive from God. He not only equalizes our pain, He also makes the pain; seem relatively insignificant. We pray the Lord's prayer daily and persistently because we are really praying for a new day of being immersed in God's Spirit. His Spirit is a gift of unimaginable value, for He reveals to us what God is up to—things our minds could never imagine.

> *These hard times are small potatoes compared to the coming good times, the lavish celebration prepared for us. There's far more here than meets the eye. The things we see now are here today, gone tomorrow. But the things we can't see now will last forever.*
> 2 Corinthians 4:17 MSG

> *That is what the Scriptures mean when they say, "No eye has seen, no ear has heard, and no mind has imagined what God has prepared for those who love Him." But it was to us that God revealed these things by His Spirit. For His Spirit searches out everything and shows us God's deep secrets.*
> I Corinthians 2:9-10 NLT

Keep Prayer Alive

Whatever you do, don't turn this prayer into a routine. Keep this prayer outline alive by being specific. Don't just tell the Lord you love Him; tell Him today why He is so lovable in your eyes.

Don't just ask for His kingdom to come; invite Him into specific situations in your life to perform His will.

Don't merely ask Him for bread. Ask Him to feed you with something from the text you just read, and then invite Him into your vocation, your relationships, and your church. Ask Him to feed you at all levels of need.

Don't just be generally forgiving; let specific things that are bothering you go, by announcing people forgiven and blessed.

Don't just generally rebuke the devil. Talk to God about what is tempting you right now. Keep prayer alive, specific, and intimate.

Scripture

Not If, but "When" We Pray

"And when you pray...." Matthew 6:5 NKJV

The Lord's Prayer Is Our Private Prayer

"But you, when you pray, go into your room, and when you have shut your door, pray to your Father Who is in the secret place...."
Matthew 6:6 NKJV

The Lord's Prayer: Not Liturgy, but Topics

"And when you pray, do not use vain repetitions as the heathen do."
Matthew 6:7 NKJV

He Calls Us to Pray in This Similar Manner

"In this manner, therefore, pray: 'Our Father'...." Matthew 6:9 NKJV

Never Give Up on Praying

Jesus told them a story, showing that it was necessary for them to pray consistently and never quit. Luke 18:1 MSG

Everything in the world is about to be wrapped up, so take nothing for granted. Stay wide-awake in prayer. 1 Peter 4:7 MSG

Passionate Prayer Is Effective Prayer

The earnest prayer of a righteous person has great power and produces wonderful results. James 5:16 NLT

Prayer Is the Christian's Response to Worry

Don't fret or worry. Instead of worrying, pray. Let petitions and praises shape your worries into prayers, letting God know your concerns. Before you know it, a sense of God's wholeness, everything coming together for good, will come and settle you down. It's wonderful what happens when Christ displaces worry at the center of your life. Philippians 4:6-7 MSG

Prayer According to God's Will

"You have not asked for anything in this way before, but now you must ask in My name. Then it will be given to you, so that you will be completely happy." John 16:24 CEV

Motives Affect Prayer

Yet even when you do pray, your prayers are not answered, because you pray just for selfish reasons. James 4:3 CEV

Confidence in Prayer Gets Results

Now this is the confidence that we have in Him, that if we ask anything according to His will, He hears us. And if we know that He hears us, whatever we ask, we know that we have the petitions that we have asked of Him. 1 John 5:14-15 NKJV

"I tell you, you can pray for anything, and if you believe that you've received it, it will be yours." Mark 11:24 NLT

Your Name Be Kept Holy

The Hebrew people, from their beginning, knew God by many different titles but by only one name: "Yahweh" or Jehovah. This name to them revealed one basic fact: God was personal to them, but His name was unknown, not even pronounceable.

Not until Moses, when he was with God at the burning bush, did God fully reveal what His name meant. It was there that Moses asked God the question, "What name can I pronounce to Israel to let them know who You are?" God told Moses that this name they had known Him by, "Yahweh," meant that He was the "I AM WHO I AM."

In essence, He was saying to Moses and His people, "I exist. I am always here and I will always be here now, in your presence." God revealed Himself as the personal God Who will never leave or forsake His people, no matter what.

That is the name we are to keep holy, separated, and reserved only for God. We declare that only God is the center of life; only Jehovah is so deeply relational that He is able to completely care for us. Only Jehovah is always now, always present.

> *But Moses protested, "If I go to the people of Israel and tell them, 'The God of your ancestors has sent me to you,' they will ask me, 'What is His name?' Then what should I tell them?" God replied to Moses, "I Am Who I Am. Say this to the people of Israel: I Am has sent me to you." God also said to Moses, "Say this to the people of Israel: 'Yahweh,' the God of your ancestors—the God of Abraham, the God of Isaac, and the God of Jacob—has sent me to you."* Exodus 3:14-15 NLT

God didn't stop there; He took this name, Jehovah, and added other words to it throughout the Bible so we could know that He would be present to work in our lives. Below are just a few examples.

JEHOVAH-TSIDKENU or "Jehovah, our righteousness": He is the One who brings us into right relationship.

JEHOVAH-M'KADDESH or "Jehovah who sanctifies": He is the One who sets us apart for great things.

JEHOVAH-SHALOM or "Jehovah is peace": He is the One who takes all our barriers away.

JEHOVAH-SHAMMAH or "Jehovah is there": He is the One who gets to where we are going before we arrive; we are never alone.

JEHOVAH-ROPHE or "Jehovah heals": He is the One who heals all our diseases.

JEHOVAH-JIREH or "God provides": He provides all we need.

Ch. 5

RPMs–Meditation

A grade school teacher was frustrating her student. The student was searching for the immediate right answer. The teacher was trying to show him how to know the answer was right by doing the equation himself. She was wearing down. It was a clash of wills, but in the end she prevailed. Finally, the boy gave up on getting the answer out of her and started asking the questions that would help him solve the problem. Through many inquiries, trials, and errors, he figured out how to get the right answer. In that simple moment, he grew from a defeated little boy to a confident young student (disciple).

During the meditation portion of the RPMs, write down the passage that grabs your attention and stands out. Then, ask questions of the passage. You do not need to ask all of the following questions. They are just ideas to help lead you to a deeper understanding of what you are reading.

1. What about this passage grabs my attention the most? What word, phrase, or sentence? Did it bring comfort to something in my heart? Did it stir hope or answer a question? Did it create an unexplainable curiosity?

2. Enter the story more fully by searching the context around the verse or passage. Make sure you know whom was being spoken to, where they were when they were spoken to, what the occasion was, and what these words would have meant to the original audience.

3. Was there anything in the passage that didn't seem to fit or belong?

4. Ask the Holy Spirit if He wishes to reveal anything to you. Does He want to bring any question to your mind?

Why All the Questions?

God wants us to ask, seek, and knock so that He might build a value in our heart for His Word. The human heart was created to search passionately for what it values. Nothing in this life is more valuable than God's Words, for His Words are the substance of our relationship with Him and the source of our faith. As we seek Scripture, we will value God and His promises more and more. When we ask questions of a passage of Scripture, we naturally turn our heart and thoughts toward God. The author of the Bible is God, so any questions (direct or indirect) begin to focus our thoughts more specifically on Him. As we focus our thoughts on God through questions, the Holy Spirit reveals Jesus (the Author of the promises), and the process of searching intensifies the value we place on God's Word.

Meditation focuses the mind on God and opens the heart to see and hear what could not be seen without the help of God. Our questions are the breeding grounds for a searching, focused, and hearing heart.

KEEP ON SEARCHING - *"Keep on asking, and you will receive what you ask for. Keep on seeking, and you will find. Keep on knocking, and the door will be opened to you. For everyone who asks, receives. Everyone who seeks, finds. And to everyone who knocks, the door will be opened."* Matthew 7:7-8 NLT

IT'S YOUR PRIVILEGE - *It is God's privilege to conceal things and the king's privilege to discover them.* Proverbs 25:2 NLT

IT'S BETTER THAN WEALTH AND PLEASURE - *God's Word is better than a diamond, better than a diamond set between emeralds. You'll like it better than strawberries in spring, better than red, ripe strawberries.* Psalm 19:10 MSG

Application - 1

Here are three simple actions that will help guide you through the meditation process:

1. Select a verse or phrase that grabs your attention the most.
2. Ask the question of God, "What does this verse or passage mean to me?"
3. Write the verse or phrase down, asking God to make sense of it in His time and in His way.

Meditation is the ability to focus on God and His Word and allow Him to speak to you from the Scripture. Meditation usually leads to the two events of insight and application.

Meditation allows our heart to hear the rumbling of the Spirit of God. We see something that we did not see at first, and then we comprehend how God wants it to affect our lives.

Two lists of Scriptures are printed below. In one list you will find the Scriptures that describe the benefits of meditation; in the other list we will discover the help of the Holy Spirit as we meditate.

Application - 2

Now that you have written down the passage that grabbed your attention and have asked, "Why do you think it caught my eye?" Probe further. Did the passage inspire hope or bring comfort? Answer questions about the passage like, "Who is being spoken to?" and "What do you think the original reader thought about when he was reading?"

As you begin to read the Scriptures in this manner, you will naturally begin to meditate. Eastern meditation seeks to empty the mind of activity, distractions, and scattered thoughts and become aware and focused on one thing. The Christ "followers" are different. They seek to be led by God to hear God speak to their thoughts. The Christian does not focus on one thing, but rather on God Who reveals Himself through His Word. *"And now, in these final days, He has spoken to us through His Son"* (Hebrews 1:2 NLT). *"The Word gave life to everything that was created, and His life brought light to everyone"* (John 1:4 NLT).

The Bible best defines what godly meditation is:

REFLECT - *I will study Your commandments and reflect on Your ways.* Psalm 119:15 NLT

ABSORB - *I'm absorbed in pondering Your wise counsel. Yes, Your sayings on life are what give me delight; I listen to them as to good neighbors!* Psalm 119:23 MSG

RELISH - *I cherish Your commandments—oh, how I love them!—relishing every fragment of Your counsel.* Psalm 119:48 MSG

PONDER - *I stayed awake all night, prayerfully pondering Your promise.* Psalm 119:148 MSG

Scripture

Meditation and Prosperity

Study this Book of Instruction continually. Meditate on it day and night so you will be sure to obey everything written in it. Only then will you prosper and succeed in all you do. Joshua 1:8 NLT

Meditation and Blessing

Oh, the joys of those who do not follow the advice of the wicked, or stand around with sinners, or join in with mockers. But they delight in the law of the Lord, meditating on it day and night.
Psalm 1:1-2 NKJV

Meditation and Memory

I will meditate on Your precepts, and contemplate Your ways. I will delight myself in Your statutes; I will not forget Your word.
Psalm 119:15-16 NKJV

Meditation, a Source For Hope

I rise before the dawning of the morning, and cry for help; I hope in Your word. My eyes are awake through the night watches, that I may meditate on Your Word. Psalm 119:147-149 NKJV

Meditation, a Way of Thinking

Finally, brethren, whatever things are true, whatever things are noble, whatever things are just, whatever things are pure, whatever things are lovely, whatever things are of good report, if there is any virtue and if there is anything praiseworthy—meditate on these things.
Philippians 4:8 NKJV

May the words of my mouth and the meditation of my heart be pleasing to You, O Lord, my Rock and my Redeemer. Psalm 19:14 NKJV

Meditation, Expressing Love

Oh, how I love Your law! It is my meditation all the day.
Psalm 119:97 NKJV

Scriptures on the Holy Spirit Helping Us Understand the Scriptures

The Holy Spirit Helps Us Interpret What God Means.

Above all, you must realize that no prophecy in Scripture ever came from the prophet's own understanding, or from human initiative. No, those prophets were moved by the Holy Spirit, and they spoke from God. 2 Peter 1:20-21 NLT

God Inspired Its Writing; He Inspires Its Interpretation

All Scripture is inspired by God and is useful to teach us what is true and to make us realize what is wrong in our lives. It corrects us when we are wrong and teaches us to do what is right. 2 Timothy 3:16 NLT

God Speaks Through His Son, Not Our Minds

Long ago, God spoke many times and in many ways to our ancestors through the prophets. And now in these final days, He has spoken to us through His Son. Hebrews 1:1-2 NLT

The Holy Spirit Teaches Us and Reminds Us of Those Things Jesus Has Taught Us

"These things I have spoken to you while being present with you. But the Helper, the Holy Spirit, whom the Father will send in My name, He will teach you all things, and bring to your remembrance all things that I said to you." John 14:25-26 NKJV

The Holy Spirit Testifies for Christ—Showing Us Jesus in His Word

*"But when the Helper comes, whom I shall send to you from the Father,
the Spirit of truth Who proceeds from the Father, He will testify of Me."*
John 15:26 NKJV

The Holy Spirit Guides Us into All Truth

*"But when the Friend comes, the Spirit of the Truth, He will take you by
the hand and guide you into all the truth there is."* John 16:13 MSG

The Holy Spirit Teaches Us What Is True, Not with a Human Explanation

*But you have received the Holy Spirit, and He lives within you, so you
don't need anyone to teach you what is true. For the Spirit teaches you
everything you need to know, and what He teaches is true….*
I John 2:27 NLT

Ch. 6

RPMs–Signature

Some years back, a brilliant and inventive man had an idea for changing the way the world recorded music. Instead of using plastic tape that had been coated with ferric oxide powder, which could then be magnetized as it passed by an electromagnetic field, he would burn a binary code onto a plastic disc that could be placed in a CD player. One would be able to purchase these players for $49.99 (up until then, expensive equipment had been required). The problem was, he had no way to turn what he knew into a mass-producing action. A couple of years later, the technology was introduced to the market without the help of the man who first figured out how to do it. He had no way to turn his insight into action. His insight was lost because he had no way to practically market it.

Insight

Meditation leads to insight. Insight is simply seeing something or thinking about something in a way that you have never before. Once an insight touches your mind, you will want to remember it. The best way to remember an insight is to write it down as briefly as you can.

When you write down what God is showing you, you're in good company. Habakkuk (one of God's prophets) was told to do the same thing so that, when life became full and intense, even on the run, he could read the will of God and know what to do.

> *What's God going to say to my questions? I'm braced for the worst. I'll climb to the lookout tower and scan the horizon. I'll wait to see what God says, how He'll answer my complaint. And then GOD answered: "Write this. Write what you see. Write it out in big block letters so that it can be read on the run. This vision-message is a witness pointing to what's coming. It aches for the coming—it can hardly wait! And it doesn't lie. If it seems slow in coming, wait. It's on its way. It will come right on time."* Habakkuk 2:1-3 MSG

The prophet goes on to imply that self-important people would never treasure God's Word enough to write it down and really understand what God was saying, but the person with a right heart would go the distance. They would write down what they saw God doing, and then they would live, really live, because basic Bible reading and meditation had just turned into complete faith in God.

> *Look at the proud! Their spirit is not right in them, but the righteous live by their faith.* Habakkuk 2:4 NRSV

Application

Application answers the questions, "How does the insight impact me? What do I sense God asking me to do in response to what I am seeing from this particular passage?" Remember, God isn't speaking to you to increase your Bible knowledge. You can take a Bible study course for that. God is interested in building your relationship with Him. You build a relationship with God through acting in faith on what He is leading you to do. As you believe and act on God's will, God builds a faith relationship with you that will revolutionize you into the person He has planned you to be.

You see the insight. You know what He wants you to do. Now it is time to get about the dangerous business of signing your name to it. Get a journal and write it down.

Signing the Insight

1. Write down the verse that grabbed your attention.
2. Write down the insight. "How does God want me to apply the passage to my life?"
3. Write a prayer to God confessing your desire to obey and requesting His grace to help.

You will want to write your insight and action step in as brief a sentence as possible. You should not expect God to give you an insight every day, but it should be frequent. The purpose of signing is to remember what God has said to you and to get serious about obeying God so that your faith relationship with Him can grow.

Abraham's Example

By an act of faith, Abraham said yes to God's call to travel to an unknown place that would become his home. When he left, he had no idea where he was going. By an act of faith, he lived in the country promised him, lived as a stranger camping in tents. Abraham did it by keeping his eye on an unseen city with real, eternal foundations—the City designed and built by God. Sometimes all we can see are the promises, but they should be enough. Hebrews 11:8 MSG

Be Careful to Obey God's Word

This is God's eternal pattern: we obey His voice by faith, and then

He moves us into the fulfillment of that promise. Abraham obeyed, not knowing exactly what the place to which he was headed was like; yet, in the end his entire family inherited what God had promised. Always keep your heart open to God's leading. Read the Scripture; observe the passage; write down the verse, insight, and action you sense God is leading you to take; and then sign in a prayer. In the end, you will watch God perform miracles as He takes you to the incredible places He has promised and multiplies your life beyond your imagination.

> *"Every commandment which I command you today you must be careful to observe, that you may live and multiply, and go in and possess the land of which the LORD swore to your fathers."*
> Deuteronomy 8:1 NKJV

When we sign the name of Jesus to the will-of-God prayers, Jesus signs our names to the answers.

Get a Journal

Personally, I use a Moleskin notebook. It fits me, but any notebook with which you are comfortable with will do. First, I write down the Scripture from the text that stood out to me. Second, I write a simple insight of how I think God may want to apply the passage to my life. Third, I write a prayer resigning my will to God's and asking for His grace to help. Fourth, I give my day a title and put it in a Table of Contents at the beginning of my notebook. That way I can recall what God has spoken to me in the past. Imagine, over a year's time you can go back and look at the themes God has been emphasizing in your heart again and again. Finally, I text or Twitter my insight to others for accountability and then read their insights to me, so I can be strengthened as we watch God lead us together.

The signing part may not seem important, but this is where you seal God's Word to your heart, give it a place in your heart, and honor God with your affections. A life that merely believes in God is not much better than a demonic life (James 2:19), but a life that hears and acts is a blessed life (James 1:21-25).

Scripture

Faith Leads to Action ... Obedience is Birthed By Faith

I can already hear one of you agreeing by saying, "Sounds good. You take care of the faith department, I'll handle the works department." Not so fast. You can no more show me your works apart from your faith than I can show you my faith apart from my works. Faith and works, works and faith, fit together hand in glove. James 2:18 MSG

Good Fruit or Actions Are the Result of Faith

"A good tree produces good fruit, and a bad tree produces bad fruit. A good tree can't produce bad fruit, and a bad tree can't produce good fruit." Matthew 7:17-18 NLT

The Kind of Faith Actions that Matter Are Actions that Express Love

For in Christ, neither our most conscientious religion nor disregard of religion amounts to anything. What matters is something far more interior: faith expressed in love. Galatians 5:6 MSG

Faith Promotes Heroic Actions

Through acts of faith, they toppled kingdoms, made justice work, took the promises for themselves. They were protected from lions, fires, and sword thrusts, turned disadvantage to advantage, won battles, routed alien armies. Women received their loved ones back from the dead.

There were those who, under torture, refused to give in and go free, preferring something better: resurrection. Others braved abuse and whips, and, yes, chains and dungeons. We have stories of those who were stoned, sawed in two, murdered in cold blood; stories of vagrants wandering the earth in animal skins, homeless, friendless, powerless— the world didn't deserve them!—making their way as best they could on the cruel edges of the world. Hebrews 11:33-35 MSG

When Faith Is Followed by Action, a Life Is Stabilized

"So then, everyone who hears My words and puts them into practice is like a wise man. He builds his house on the rock." Matthew 7:24 NIRV

Part 3

How Will Reading Scripture Profit?

Ch. 7

Jesus Faith

When I first began my journey with Christ, faith was code for believing in the doctrine or teachings of the Bible. As I have continued with Christ, that concept of faith has been smashed.

Imagine a little boy huddled in a corner. Towering over him is his angry dad, ready to strike the boy for trampling some newly planted flowers he had told him to stay away from. Make no mistake, the son huddled in fear completely believes that his dad is his dad and that he should have stayed clear of the flower bed.

Now, imagine another son and a different family. The son was told not to use his father's tools. The son did as he pleased and made quick toys of them. His father sits him down to talk it through, but there is no fear in this son. Why? Because this son trusts his dad's love and care for him— he is free of fear. Both sons likely believed in their dads and what their dads had told them to do. One, however, was full of fear, and the other was not. Why?

Jesus Redefines Faith

Jesus redefined words so people could comprehend God's truths with greater depth. One example is the word "faith." He made faith mean something much deeper than mere mental agreement or assent ("I agree that such a thing exists or happened"). Many people affirm or give mental assent to truths about Christ, and yet they remain, for the most part, unchanged. Why? Because assent or affirmation alone is not life-transforming.

Two Words that Define Faith

Faithfulness

The first word to describe faith is "fidelity," or "faithfulness," which is the opposite of idolatry (or infidelity). Idolatry is giving your heart, or the center of your affection, to someone other than God. Fidelity or faithfulness is giving your heart fully to Christ.

When two people get married, they give themselves to each other exclusively. If either mate violates that relationship, then trust or faith is broken. Faith in Christ does not just mean to believe that He exists or is real, but to entrust your life to Him in an exclusive way.

In John 3:16, we are called upon to "believe in Him" or to remain faithful in relationship to Him. *"For God loved the world so much that He gave His one and only Son, so that everyone who believes in Him will not perish but have eternal life"* (NLT).

God loves us so much that He brings us into eternal life through a relationship of fidelity with His Son Jesus. It actually requires little mental affirmation to believe that Jesus exists or that He lived, died, and rose from the dead. The evidence is so overwhelming. It does require, however, our entire heart to be full of faith and faithful to God.

Trust

The second word to describe faith has a credible thought—to "trust," which refers to the complete and full confidence you place in another. Our relationship with God is not only one of fidelity, but also one of complete trust.

The opposite of trust (logically) seems to be mistrust, yet Jesus went deeper and claimed the opposite of trust was anxiety. To not trust God is to actually be anxious. *"I tell you not to worry about everyday life—whether you have enough food and drink,…. Can all your worries add a single moment to your life? …. And why worry about your clothing? …. So don't worry about these things, saying, 'What will we eat? What will we drink? What will we wear?' …. So don't worry about tomorrow…."* (Matthew 6:25, 27, 28, 31, 34 CEV).

To lack trust is to doubt—not to doubt or question statements about God, but to doubt or question God's love and care for you. *"And if God cares so wonderfully for wildflowers that are here today and thrown into the fire tomorrow, He will certainly care for you. Why do you have so little faith?"* (Matthew 6:30 NLT) Having "little faith" is being anxious about God's care; genuine faith completely trusts in God's love and care.

As you can see, mental-assent faith believes or agrees with certain facts about someone or something. Fidelity-faith or trust-faith is relational faith. It is the kind of faith that remains true to the priority of Jesus' being at the center of the heart's affection.

In order for our hearts to be lost in faith, our hearts must also be lost in love. Faith is trusting the one you love and being faithful to that same person. It is one thing to know that Jesus is Lord and that He has given us Himself and Scripture as the authority over our lives. It is another thing to place our faith in Him, to trust Him, and to be faithful to Him.

Above all else, the reading of Scripture is an act of deep love and devotion. When a love relationship is formed with our Father, we are no longer cowering little children huddled in a corner awaiting our Father's terror. We are His children trusting in His care. To believe in God on your own could create within you a deep sense of terror and damaging fear toward God. To believe in God the way Christ gifts us to believe in Him makes us both faithful and trusting in our relationship.

Scriptures

It Will Be Done to Me According to My Faith

When He had gone indoors, the blind men came to Him, and He asked them, "Do you believe that I am able to do this?" "Yes, Lord," they replied. Then He touched their eyes and said, "According to your faith will it be done to you'; and their sight was restored.
Matthew 9:29-30 NIV

Faith Makes Nothing Impossible to Me

When the disciples had Jesus off to themselves, they asked, "Why couldn't we throw it out?" "Because you're not yet taking God seriously," said Jesus. The simple truth is that if you had a mere kernel of faith, a poppy seed, say, you would tell this mountain, 'Move!' and it would move. There is nothing you wouldn't be able to tackle."
Matthew 17:19-21 MSG

I Do Greater Things by Faith

"I tell you the truth, anyone who believes in Me will do the same works I have done, and even greater works, because I am going to be with the Father. You can ask for anything in My name, and I will do it, so that the Son can bring glory to the Father." John 14:12-13 NLT

Faith in Jesus Makes Me Strong

"By faith in the name of Jesus, this man whom you see and know was made strong." Acts 3:16 NIV

I Am Accepted by God on the Basis of Faith

The good news tells how God accepts everyone who has faith, but only those who have faith. It is just as the Scriptures say, "The people God accepts because of their faith will live." Romans 1:16-17 TEV

All That Matters Is the Kind of Faith That Makes Me Love

If you are a follower of Christ Jesus, it makes no difference whether you are circumcised or not. All that matters is your faith that makes you love others. Galatians 5:6 CEV

God Is Worthy of My Faith

Give all your worries and cares to God, for He cares about you.
I Peter 5:7 NLT

Give your burdens to the Lord, and He will take care of you. He will not permit the godly to slip and fall. Psalm 55:22 NLT

Since God assured us, "I'll never let you down, never walk off and leave you," we can boldly quote, God is there, ready to help; I'm fearless no matter what. Who or what can get to me? Hebrews 13:5-6 MSG

Ch. 8

Growing Faith

If trust and faithfulness are at the heart of Christ's definition of faith, how do I grow in faith? How can I make my faith stronger so that it can be the force in my life that God intends it to be?

Picture a father returning home after a hard day at work. First, he kisses his wife, who is busy cooking dinner, and then he's off to the bedroom to see his son. There his son sits, engrossed with a computer game, "Combat Grounds." The dad attempts a conversation, but his son is too absorbed. The dad expresses an interest in his son's game, but again, the son is too occupied to be disturbed. Finally, the father asks the son if he would like to go outside and shoot a few hoops. His son remains oblivious.

Faith is powerful, for it frees us from self-preoccupation, anxiety, self-doubt, and insecurity. It is the only ingredient of heart and spirit that frees us to live for what is transcendent. The son can't break away from what has captured him, just like we sometimes struggle to break away from what captures us. Our entire culture is consumed with pursuing feelings. Feelings are the utopia. We want to feel good about everything in life. When pain approaches, we search for drugs, entertainment, gambling, shopping, food, porn, sex, religion, and a slew of other things that instantly gratify.

Christ's whole point was that things don't satisfy. They just keep us searching. However, once we drink from His eternal fountain, we need never search again. Our entire relationship with God is built on faith. Our inner power to depart from obsession with feelings to relational fulfillment depends on a faith relationship with Christ. It's not a mental agreement with His existence and teaching, but faithfulness toward Him and complete trust in His leading and care. If this kind of faith is so important, how does one come by it and how does it grow?

Growing in Faith

Faith does not magically appear in the heart; it is formed there. The Bible says it is formed as one listens to God's Word. This is not as easy as it might sound because the sender and the receiver must understand the same information for listening to actually occur. That is why God made sure we would understand what He was saying by giving us His Word to read and listen.

When a follower has listened to God's Word over and over again, His voice is easier to detect, discern, and interpret. As we read about Him and talk to Him, we begin to understand Him. Eventually, the Holy Spirit will come and talk to your heart about certain things, about acting in particular ways and going specific places. When He does, faith will already be in your heart because faith grows as you listen to God's Word. God's Word gives us the ability to discern the voice of the Holy Spirit, as we are being led to do things the Bible does not entirely address.

It works like this: we listen to God's Word, faith grows, a faithful trust relationship with God is formed, and we are transformed into a new person.

> So faith comes from hearing the Good News, and people hear the Good News when someone tells them about Christ. Romans 10:17 NCV

> Before you trust, you have to listen. Romans 10:17 MSG

The more I listen to God's voice, the more my faith grows. Trust, confidence, and fidelity toward Christ increase. Instead of anxiety consuming my heart and decisions, God fills me with great hope and expectations in what He has to say. I like to say it like this: faith is picking a fight with my destiny, demanding that, rather than submitting itself to my natural inclinations, it submit to the power of God's Word. God's Word is creative, powerful, and sustaining. When His Word lives in my heart, I greatly grow in faith.

Sheep and Faith

God used the shepherd and sheep relationship to depict our fidelity and our trust relationship with Him. Why sheep? Because sheep are completely dependent, and to survive they must be faithful to follow the voice of their shepherd. If you want to really grow as a disciple, then here are three key traits you will want to pay attention to: *"My sheep a)* **listen to My voice** *b)* **I know them,** *and c)* **they follow Me.** *I give them eternal life, and they will never perish. No one can snatch them away from Me"* (John 10:26-28 NLT; emphasis mine).

a) "LISTEN TO MY VOICE"—as Jesus speaks to us.

All relationship is built on listening, and if we want to really be faithful and trust in Christ, we must deeply listen to Him—not merely read His Word, but listen as He speaks to us as we read His Word. All listening has a qualification—honor. We must honor God and His Word if we are going to listen to Him. If we don't honor God and His Word, we will place no value on listening to what He has to say. This is why the first commandment is toward God and has to do with our honor of Him. *"You shall have no other God...."* (Exodus 20:3). That is why the greatest and most important commandment deals with honoring God by loving Him with your whole heart (Matthew 22:37), and that is why the first command with a promise is to honor parents (Ephesians 6:2). When you do not honor someone, you will not listen to him or her. In the case of God, if you do not honor, you will not listen, and if you do not listen, you will have no faith. If you have no faith, you will have no relationship with God.

We might assume faith comes from listening, but really, faith comes from honoring God enough to listen.

b) "I KNOW THEM"—as He opens our hearts and shows us what's going on inside.

Listening to God's Word creates an unusual phenomenon. It opens our hearts and allows God to show us what's inside. Most people get real edgy when they think about opening their hearts and letting Jesus see and then reveal to them what He see. That view of God is tragic. No doubt, God does show those things that are damaging us, but more importantly, God is eager to reveal our potential: what we could be, what our hearts long to be. The reason God exposes the evil within is that the evil within is keeping us from being all we can be. The Word of God has a powerful ability to open us up and reveal our hearts to us with inspiring accuracy (Hebrews 4:12).

c) "THEY FOLLOW ME"—Who wouldn't, after God has shown us who we are and Who He is?

When we have heard God's Word, and when we allow Him to show us our hearts, we naturally follow. Who wouldn't want to take off after a God Who has revealed such an amazing future based on His unbreakable promises?

Scriptures

My Life Is Built to Withstand Storms As I Listen to God's Word

"Anyone who hears and obeys these teachings of Mine is like a wise person who built a house on solid rock. Rain poured down, rivers flooded, and winds beat against that house. But it did not fall, because it was built on solid rock." Matthew 7:24-25 CEV

Joy Is Built in My Heart As I Listen to God's Word

Jesus replied, "That's true, but the people who are really blessed are the ones who hear and obey God's message!" Luke 11:28 CEV

God's Word Penetrates and Probes Every Part of My Life, Helping Me to Listen to God

His powerful Word is sharp as a surgeon's scalpel, cutting through everything, whether doubt or defense, laying us open to listen and obey. Nothing and no one is impervious to God's Word. We can't get away from it—no matter what. Hebrews 4:12 MSG

God Works in My Heart As I Listen to His Word

And now we look back on all this and thank God, an artesian well of thanks! When you got the Message of God we preached, you didn't pass it off as just one more human opinion, but you took it to heart as God's true word to you, which it is, God Himself at work in you believers!
 1 Thessalonians 2:13 MSG

Our Life Comes from the Eternal Word of God

For you have been born again, but not to a life that will quickly end. Your new life will last forever because it comes from the eternal, living word of God. I Peter 1:23 NLT

Ch. 9

Daily Faith

One of the greatest challenges of my early Christian life was the steady approach to reading Scripture. I could study for a class, read a book, and read the Word to prepare for a message, but I often found myself skipping devotions. I hope it is clear by now that Christ and His Scriptures are our authority, and when we come under authority, we receive authority (Luke 7:8-9).

Why the Struggle to Read Daily?

So why the struggle with daily feeding my soul on the Word of God, when only success and prosperity will result? Many answers exist, but to those serious about following Jesus, I think the answer is simple. We assume that missing a day or two here and there won't have any kind of a significant impact. The problem is that our appetite never knows when to stop. Once we feed a desire, our desires take over and turn reckless. Every huge problem in life starts tiny—one more drink, one small flirty text, a few more harsh words to win the argument. It is always the little things that transform into the big. Cars without brakes can be deadly. Maybe the hill doesn't look that steep, but once you have committed to descend it, loss of control can be immediate. When you have no brakes, it can turn fatal. Souls without authority can become deadly. Once we begin a day or two of neglect, a month or two of absence can result. Without brakes, we are left racing downhill with only disaster as a destiny.

Absent Faith Can Be Fatal

To be absent of faith can be fatal to our eco-spiritual system. Notice how Paul puts it: *"For 'whoever calls on the name of the Lord shall be saved.' How then shall they call on Him in whom they have not believed?"* (Romans 10:13-14 NKJV)

If we do not call on the Lord, how can we be saved? The word "saved" here means "to be made whole or to be healed" or "to be kept safe from danger." Paul is asking the question, how can we have a whole heart apart from prayer? If you were raised in a broken home, if you have been through a divorce, if you have been abused on any levelor have experienced a trauma, participated in an addiction, or become harsh and indifferent through a self-righteous spirit, your heart has been broken into a number of pieces and you are slowly dying on the inside. How do you expect to get well when medicine and psychology will not work in the places where you are really sick and hurting? What about the part of you that only God can heal, that only God can touch? How will you be healed unless you invite Him in to do the healing? He won't just barge in.

Paul goes further. How will you ask Him if you don't have faith? In order to genuinely ask, faith must be present, and faith is the gift God gives us as we listen to His Gospel, His Word. *"So then faith comes by hearing, and hearing by the Word of God"* (Romans 10:17 NKJV). A few days of skipping devotions, how can it hurt? Then all of a sudden, I discover there are no brakes and I can't stop what I have started. The Word is absent from my life, and faith is non-existent. There is no ability to pray when I find myself fatally sick. As you can see, absent faith can be fatal to my spiritual eco-system.

A college student attended a required history course at a university. He never missed a class, took copious notes, turned in all assignments, and listened intently to the lecturer. He did, however, neglect to read the assigned textbook and skipped the personal appointment with the presiding professor. Finally, the end of the term arrived along with the final essay exam. The test questions were largely drawn from the textbook and the ability to comprehend the larger intricacies of specific historical events. I wonder, how wise was the college student for skipping his daily readings of the textbook?

Life is full of tests. Indeed, they are coming. The goal is to be daily read up so that you have the right answer to every life test–"faith"– complete fidelity and trust toward God. This is not just a mental-assent faith, but a faith that has taken you to the feet of Jesus, causing you to cry out with a full heart, "I trust You, and I delight in being faithful or full of faith in all circumstances. Feed me Your Word as I read today."

How and Why Should We Read Scripture?

The best way to hear God's Word and grow a faith relationship is by reading Scripture daily. As we read, it becomes easier to hear His voice, and hearing His voice is where faith relationship begins (Romans 10:17). The Scripture itself gives us clear and highly motivating reasons to read Scripture.

A MATTER OF DEVOTION — The first Christians devoted themselves to God's Word by listening to it through the apostles. The word "devoted" means "to give constant and diligent attention to." *"All the believers devoted themselves to the apostles' teaching"* (Acts 2:42 NLT). The success of the early church to establish followers worldwide depended on their relationship to God's Word. In fact, the first book that chronicles the birth of the Church is called "Acts." The book describes how Jesus guided, built, and prospered His church through His Holy Spirit. Imagine, the early Christians succeeded in life by the empowering of the Holy Spirit, and the Holy Spirit led them to be devoted to God's Word in the apostles' teaching. Those apostles who once taught God's Word wrote the Scriptures so that we could read them. Without a doubt, the Holy Spirit calls upon us to read God's Word as a matter of devotion so faith can grow in us. As we do, "Acts" of the Holy Spirit will continue to be performed.

A MATTER OF EXCELLENCE — Some early Christians were considered noble, or more excellent of spirit and character, because they daily searched Scripture. *"And the people of Berea were more open-minded than those in Thessalonica, and they listened eagerly to Paul's message. They searched the Scriptures day after day to see if Paul and Silas were teaching the truth"* (Acts 17:11 NLT). This is how faith, great faith, is formed deeply into the heart, seeking out what God has really said.

A MATTER OF STABILITY — Jesus' promise: "Build your life on My Word, and you will stand in storms and difficulty." *"Anyone who listens to My teaching and follows it is wise, like a person who builds a house on solid rock. Though the rain comes in torrents and the floodwaters rise and the winds beat against that house, it won't collapse because it is built on bedrock"* (Matthew 7:24-25 NLT). The Word of God does its best work in hearts that have been shattered by storms and difficulties.

A MATTER OF FREEDOM — Jesus promises that the truth will set you free—not just any truth, but the truth you know will set you free. We read the Word to know the truth that will set us free. *"Jesus said to the people who believed in Him, 'You are truly My disciples if you remain faithful to My teachings. And you will know the truth, and the truth will set you free'"* (John 8:31-32 NLT).

A MATTER OF FAVOR—When we discover God's Word, we also discover God's favor—power to live in His strength and with His joy. *"Listen to my instruction and be wise. Don't ignore it. Joyful are those who listen to me, watching for me daily at my gates, waiting for me outside my home! For whoever finds me finds life and receives favor from the Lord"* (Proverbs 8:33-35 NLT).

A MATTER OF PROSPERITY—As we study God's word and grow in faith, we will be prosperous and succeed. *"Study this Book of Instruction continually. Meditate on it day and night so you will be sure to obey everything written in it. Only then will you prosper and succeed in all you do"* (Joshua 1:8 NLT).

Scripture

Keeping Your Affections Single-Focused

How can a young person stay pure? By obeying Your Word.
Psalm 119:9 NLT

Keeping Sin Conquered

I treasure Your Word above all else; it keeps me from sinning against You. Psalm 119:11 CEV

Keeping Me on the Right Path

By Your words I can see where I'm going; they throw a beam of light on my dark path. Psalm 119:105 MSG

God's Word Sustains

Jesus answered by quoting Deuteronomy: "It takes more than bread to stay alive. It takes a steady stream of words from God's mouth."
Matthew 4:4 MSG

God's Word Prospers

It is the same with My word. I send it out, and it always produces fruit. It will accomplish all I want it to, and it will prosper everywhere I send it. Isaiah 55:11 NLT

God's Word Endures

"The sky and the earth won't last forever, but My words will."
Matthew 24:35 CEV

God's Word Is Prophetic

Declaring the end from the beginning, and from ancient times things that are not yet done, saying, "My counsel shall stand, and I will do all My pleasure." Isaiah 46:10 NKJV

God's Word Is Pure

The words of the LORD are pure words, like silver tried in a furnace of earth, purified seven times. Psalm 12:6 NKJV

God's Word Is a Fire

"Does not My word burn like fire?" says the Lord.
Jeremiah 23:29 NLT

God's Word Is a Hammer

"Is it not like a mighty hammer that smashes a rock to pieces?"
Jeremiah 23:29 NLT

God's Word Is a Sword

And take the sword of the Spirit, which is the word of God.
Ephesians 6:17 NLT

God's Word Is a Surgeon's Scalpel

His powerful Word is sharp as a surgeon's scalpel, cutting through everything, whether doubt or defense, laying us open to listen and obey. Nothing and no one is impervious to God's Word. We can't get away from it—no matter what. Hebrews 4:12 MSG

Conclusion

A few years back, I wanted to increase my cadence when riding my bike. For a couple of months, I sought to boost my rpms, but I couldn't make the faster spins feel natural. I would, when not concentrating, go back to a cadence to which my body had become accustomed over so many years of riding. At first, I thought I was too old to change. Like every other aging adult, I soon denied such a foolish thought and moved my training indoors to a stationary bike. For three weeks, I rode that bike for an hour plus every day, staring at the odometer, making certain I never allowed myself to go under my desired goal, no matter how it made me feel. I didn't set the computer to do anything but keep me on the simulated flat terrain that the stationary bike allowed. I never increased or decreased the bike's resistance. One terrain, one resistance level, and one cadence for what became over twenty-four hours of riding. At the end of the three weeks, my cadence was changed, and to this day going any slower feels unnatural.

God has given us His Word. It was good enough for Jesus to use to guide and feed His life, so it should be good enough for me. As you begin to read using RPMs, it might not feel natural. I encourage you to take three or four weeks and try it. See what will at first come from your seeking to increase your revolutions around Christ in this manner. It might not feel comfortable or natural, but seek to stick with it until you form that groove of habit.

Most of all, read until faith is born in your heart—not the kind of faith that believes in what you are reading, but the kind of faith that seeks to be faithful to God, trusting where He will lead you through His Word.

In over thirty years, I have never regretted reading my Bible. I have never been disappointed. I have never been misled. I have never been deceived as I have come to God's Word seeking answers from Christ. Not one time in all the days I have read has He been a disappointment to me.

Beyond having never regretted reading my Bible, I must admit that I am more passionate about its content than ever before. I pastor and teach, not as a vocation, but as one who is still a satisfied customer. I couldn't be more elated to know and serve Christ the Lord. I pray that God will feed you to the fullest as you take personal responsibility to consume His Word daily.